MYRIAD EXPRESSIONS

Yours and Mine

Sarayu O Sringeri

BookLeaf Publishing

MYRIAD EXPRESSIONS: Yours and Mine

Presentation by *BookLeaf Publishing*

Web: www.bookleafpub.com

E-mail: info@bookleafpub.com

ISBN: 978-93-5769-838-2

First edition 2023

To Mom and Dad

PREFACE

SOS Note #1

This poetry ensemble gives a glimpse of my sojourn with poems. It has a few of the first poems I ever wrote as a little girl of 11 to some of my recent favourites. I personally feel that a poem must always be left to the reader for their own singular interpretations, for it is one of the few arts which can assume myriad forms but at the same time exist firmly in the physical realm. So I hope the title 'Myriad Expressions' holds true and your imaginations testify its worth.

INDEX

Poem I
Reminiscence

As I was walking down the street,
For a sojourn of good felt leisure,
I saw many birds in a fleet,
Returning home from their meanderings, full of pleasure.

The picture of my school flashed into my mind.
The homely blue walls and the trees, kind.
The great big field where we kids shined.
And our cosy classrooms where knowledge was intertwined.

We rushed through the gates as the sun dawned.
As though lured inwards by a magic wand.
Some clutched a book while some clutched a bat.
Everyone in their own field was a skilful acrobat.

Then the school bell rang ting a ting ting.
We stood in rows and lines as we had a prayer to sing.

Trotted, then we, back to our classes
Our teachers had to teach us- lads and lasses.

First came math, and we soldiered on
With a paper and pen, as numbers swarmed.
And then we saw it was not too bad
Thrilling and easy to befriend.

Social science was next to come,
Where we learnt the lie of the land
History, geography and economics,
Oh! How we enjoyed those debates on politics.

Science came next with its formulae
Numbers and diagrams and equations to say
It was, without doubt, our thinking alliance
Who knows who among us may be ones of
science!

English was our constant delight,
Coleridge and Shakespeare were in constant
sight
In our language classes, we saw our heritage,
Of discipline and culture, it gave us a colorful
plumage!

At the end of the day, we charged towards the
main field,
Like how a deer would run away from pursuit

As balls slid through the baskets,
Across the field were swung bats and racquets.

Now I look back and see how colorful each day was.
Every second spent was like a diamond in a treasure box.
What it has given us, our school, I have no words to say,
We hope to make it proud with every passing day.

Poem 2

Chai With The Carnations

The kettle was ready,
I pulled out a little teabag
And in she went,
Into my pretty turquoise glass.
I bathed her all over, with water, piping hot;
And perfumed her,
With honey, finest bought
Then took her out to the garden
She had to meet someone;
Those origamied carnations,
Of whom I was fond a ton.
Today they were decked in deep maroon!
I blew the steam from my tea,
To go and wish them good noon
Placed I, my blue cup, beneath the petalled beauties;
So I could grab my pencil, and get on with my poetry.

Poem 3
Morning Madness

I was walking on a road of rainbow,
And were tiny dewdrops falling upon my brow.
Then I heard a screeching noise,
I turned back to see whose was that voice.

Suddenly, I got a powerful shove,
I fell over and almost tore my glove.
I discovered the road was soft and cozy,
To get up and walk, I was a bit too lazy.

I then heard a voice say 'wake up' 'wake up'
I thought a fairy had come up.
I gave a loud sigh,
And slowly opened my eye.

I hoped for a sky full of stars or a sweet little
candy man,
But I saw my roof, bare, with a fan.
This was the end of my dream,
With me in my bed having bread and cream.

SOS Note #2

This poem was about how I vented frustration when my routine was being disciplined at the age of 12

Poem 4

Phoenix- Born From The Fire

There was a time when hope was lost
Serenity and love had no cost
A land was tossed to cruel hands,
Where spite and malice ran errands
So the motherland had to play her game,
To rise like a phoenix from the flame!

Her children toiled day and night
To take their mother from dark to light.
There were slips and flips and great blunders
By the denizens to escape the plunder
But for them, the time finally came,
To rise like a phoenix from the flames!

Patriotism was their intense fire
That made their flinty despot tire
Triumph and gaiety resurrected again
Scouring the people of their pain
The world emblazoned the country's name
For rising like a phoenix from the flame!

SOS Note #3

Written on the Independence day of 2017

Poem 5
Sprouts

Hear me out, I am a sprout!
If I am in you, you're healthy no doubt.
So listen to your mothers and eat me every day,
So that less often in your bed you lay,

Me and a frown are in constant touch,
A close friendship it is, it'll never budge.
It's a friendship greater than yours with chocolate fudge,
Still, you can ignore me not, as your mother is the judge!

SOS Note #4

One of my first poems I wrote for my school magazine after an evidently healthy lunch.

Poem 6
Treats Of Nature

Once I was done with my chores, a ton
Out went I to greet the sun
Pansies lazed in the garden with leaves undone,
While the coconut tree squealed "I'm
twenty-one"
Nature sings a song of hues
Can you comprehend- it's up to you

The jasmine blooms were up the arch
And beneath was an ant regiment march
The nightingale serenaded from the meandering
branch,
Of melodious tunes, it was a sweet avalanche
Nature sings a song of hues,
Can you fathom- it's up to you

The apple tree with a green dome
Is where the honey-lipped birds roam
Know, that if you feel a sting of stress,
This is where you ought to rest.
Nature sings a song of hues,
Can you understand-it's up to you

Poem 7
I'll Be There For You

We met with a smile and a shake of hand,
Started a journey, not knowing where we'll land.
We shared notes and split our lunch
Sometimes our prattles ended with a punch
We strolled stealthily through the corridors, long
Team projects, to the last minute, we would
prolong
Perhaps we don't see each other, as often as we
would,
But for each other, we'll be there, is what has
stood.

SOS Note #5

Penned after reminiscing times with my school friends.

Poem 8
Go

It's painful and sometimes gruelling,
You fail, you cannot go on and your dreams you feel like selling.
Journey seems worthless, you want to go away
'I will go on' is what resilience has to say
It makes you get up, it makes you take a breath,
It makes you face the stones cast by life and death.
When you move against the wind, with this virtue in your heart,
Each step is a victory, your feats manifest as art.

Poem 9
The Painting Called Nature

I went to see a golden view,
Of a living painting filled with majestic hue.
Its exotic redolence made me sink,
Into an ocean of perfume interlink.

The beautiful butterflies frisking in the brink,
In the stadium of soothing rose pink
Viewing this scene made me think,
What a great time they're having in their
upbring.

Following my enchanting stopover,
With my hand full of freshly picked clover,
Thought that there is no magic,
Than a stimulating perspective of colours
strategic
Which makes you think there is no end to
beauty.

SOS Note #6

For some reason, it appears I have written more nature poems than expected. Brace yourself

Poem 10
In Arms With Sunset

As we strolled through the golden-rimmed beach,
With eyes on the horizon, leaning to reach
In the air soared the white albatross', flaunting their pinions
Down came reigning, the white sails in water vermilion
Saw nature's winsome colours in a single frame,
Such that even a thousand human bustles couldn't tame.
All present senses, drenched in sublime bliss,
Never could you, this scene remiss.

Poem II
Anxiety

I recall the morn when,
I began to hide from sun's warm rays,
Rising became a chore, so trying,
And any form of audience became a bore.
Can I do it, perhaps not
I asked over and over, till my thoughts had clot
Anything novel became a fear,
Was it dread of failure?
Or something deep, unknown and unclear.
I was at war, every second,
A fiery duel between my senses and reason
Tears replaced blood, in this frey,
And, oh! It flowed in plenty-
Siphoning me off the last bit of zest.
Of course, I recall the morn when,
To the world, I had a smile to feign.

Poem 12
For Nothing Was Told

A truth, deep, was made
It was strung in two souls
The same truth, twinned and lived
Wrestling, unable to live suppressed and apart.
Looking for an escape to meet
The lips were savage,
Both making an unbreakable gate
For they cherished the world that valued pride,
But sadly, pride was, by that truth despised.
Despite, by heart, pleas innumerable,
Pride didn't budge
Thus, fated were the truths,
To never make a rendezvous.
All they could do was find solace,
Seeing each other from afar,
By the windows lent by kind eyes.
Unclouded, true and pure.

Poem 13
Train Journey

It bellowed,
You lurch back and forth,
And as your eyes sight the canvas of the window,
The moving wheels blend colours unknown,
To works of art never seen before.
Smiles exchanged and rendezvous made,
You can't deny, it's a moving masquerade!
Is there music? Of course there is,
And literature finest, to roam your mind's premise.
That journey can be relished, in silence and chaos,
Whether to mingle, or else,
There's no rule, no clause.
Pleasurable maybe, but undeniably short,
But at close, it offers a new odyssey to start.

SOS Note #7

Of the many journeys I have made, I would venture that train travel is most enthralling and eye-opening.

Poem 14
Strength

I live in all, I leave none
If you know I am with you, consider you've won
Though I give power, sometimes I tend to hide,
Clouded I am when there is fear, hubris and
pride.
If you keep me in your arms, you'll forget me
soon,
And if I house your mind, I'll grow to a
typhoon.
Keep me in your heart, I shall keep it pure,
Any struggle or trial you shall surely endure.

Poem 15
Black eye

Dark, merged to my being,
Branded a name, by an imperfect other,
No more wiser, and kinder less than I
Knew then, what it felt to be wronged.
Impressions mine, timid maybe,
But they do live, yearning to be lauded and seen.
Gilded in gold they may be,
But, alas, unless they appease,
The brutish select of power,
That gold, finest, shall be throttled,
Curtailed and decreased to scrap,
By the iron scythes of conceit.
Down with all! I may not be strong!
But deny me not the place where I belong.
Harsh is the remedy, to my dismay,
For all to do is pray for reason to prevail.

Poem 16
He Who Made Nature

I want to meet that artist
He does not belong to this world for sure,
For it is beyond the mindscape of earthly mortals,
To birth art of such impossible perfection,
And not just chance are his works, Like the time aided sole successes of few.
Every moment, every instance,
He grants his creations to our world
Each, the picture of grace and serenity connate.
The opulence of this soil, the knowledge in the air we breathe,
Unbelievably the work of one.
I want to meet the artist
Who's feats I may not comprehend
But can just stand afar and dote.

SOS Note #8

Written on the terrace, when one look of green has you overcome with tranquil.

Poem 17
Gratitude

Look at yourself, and answer me
Is every part of you,
A work of your own artistry?
A fool's reply would be a pompous yes
Clearly blinded,
To what world to him had blessed
I'll tell you how you're nothing,
Just a mural, colours added by ones yours and world's elements
Your beauty is your nurturer's alms
Wit yours, accorded by the wise men around
Taught trust and love by your comrades
And humility, hunger and penury,
By the waltz of world's laws and nature's rare smile.
All these and more, took you to your height,
Avail them to rise,
But forget not to revere!

SOS Note #9

Simple, but one of my favourites of the lot

Poem 18

An Unthinkable Fate

Utterly surprising, and foolishly painful it feels,
To be made aware
Of how impressionable our little heart is.
It is, but a little child
Curious to venture into uncharted paths,
Not heeding the warns of sense or knowledge
And as is known to all,
An infant learns to walk with care, only
After many a bruised knee
Not too different is the gullible heart
For it is only after the scars of heartbreaks and betrayals,
It learns to steady itself over time.
But there is one major difference of note,
Though the bruised skin is bested by time,
The scars of the heart stand undefeated.
Unyielding and returning to memory
Souring experiences, ridding one of the powers to dare.
Unscathed hearts rejoice, though you may be few
For unlike many, you have escaped a most unthinkable fate.

SOS Note #10

Have any of you readers escaped this unthinkable fate?

Poem 19
The Moon

A pearl
She shone in the plain ocean of shade deepest
Singular, radiant
She was the prize, most coveted
By ones at distance from her world
She was the muse of loving hearts
And the bane to those whom dark was dear.
She released torment, somehow
By a mere look, her kind shine
Thought not knowing not the myriad ails of
millions beneath,
She leaves sometimes, but returns
Brighter to seeking eyes, every time
Besting any anthropogenic light ever born.
She serenades music, in a language she made up
Not surprised I am that the language sounds
different,
To every soul.
For it is only unsullied love, that can savour it,
understand it and revere it.

SOS Note #11

When the street lights decide to leave the night sky alone, you can’t help but pick the pen.

Poem 20
Time

With you, every moment
Yet, like a thief, it flees
Stealing you, even as you read this
Taking you closer to your final day
And now you are helpless
Hence intensifies, the urge to hold on
Nonetheless, it's beyond;
The most powerful gods and powerful devils
It shall never wait, never look back
It seems to be the only, who hopes to see the infinite,
Shows you're midget and momentary,
Just a mirage, in time's guileful play
It is your power, your weakness
Forced, you are, to prove your worth,
In the cruelly brief span granted.
Finally, after thoughts deep,
Before this paradox, you bow before you sleep.

SOS Note #12

You stare at the clock and think.

Poem 21
Asked To Write By Else

Every time
It was my mind, own
That spoke
Every time ink stole white off the paper
My heart, feeding the words to my fingers,
My eyes closed, reminiscing and making utopia
But not today,
When my words were far away
And the sunlight of my thoughts was clouded by the disarray of present,
Another mind inspired,
Inspired to not let my ink dry,
And allowed me to borrow its words.
I took them
And I clayed them
To the sculpture I had hoped to make today.
It was different, truly
Because it was not solely my own
There was an impostor today,
Who came and added new colours
Colours I was unaware of
But I think it looked beautiful.

Poem 22
Something Along The Lines Of

Each of them, born of different shades,
Of unlike lengths and unique grace
Some have blemishes, some do not,
Some so delightful, it's hard not to spot
Couple of them tender, few of them rough,
But each has their own use, sure enough!
Albeit their origin, they come together to stay,
Their myriad tones putting up a prismatic ballet
Through their line of life, as some tend to slack,
They have nothing to fret, as they have each other's backs!
By sharing what they have through life and laugh, they have no loss or pain
They brighten and liven the eyes that view, through sun, wind and rain!

SOS Note #13

Ekphrastic poem on Annie Khun's 'Sunline'.

Poem 23

The Berry And The Girl

Away in the dark woods, lone
Nestled in the arms of green-blooded angels,
Were little hued balls of sugar grown.
Oblivious and young, they were
Not playing host to anyone but bees and the little inchworm
One day they found a new touch
It was tender, and it ferried them
To a delicate cloth-lined trug
The berries saw the fresh sky, the sun wishing them luck
For their sojourn with the girl, who had them plucked
As their little jaunt came to a close,
The girl bent down, and asked them not to be morose
She said she had a plan, for every one of them
And promised that her deft hands, would hone them into gems!
Some befriended honey, and adorned golden pancakes
While some simmered to a jam,
And with the scones were gelled to bake

The berries cherished their sweet new guise
The girl smiled, as that was her greatest prize!

SOS Note #14

Ironically, written after a failed attempt at making jam.

Poem 24
The Girl, the Merchant, the Mangoes

Alone, along a barren street
A dozen sat in woven cane;
Of mangoes, yellow, ripe and sweet,
And a girl with the sharpest brain

Why was it barren, you may ask
Or why was the lass playing seller;
The time was such that all had masked,
And no school free to venture.

But there was a silver screen, in every other home,
Before which children leaned, to have their skills honed

She couldn't have this comfort, that little girl with mangoes
In such a hard time, with not a spare dime,
What could she do or where could she go?

On the very same day, there walked a tradesman there;
In him he had kindness and to offer he had care!
As his eyes met the vendor, he walked to her and asked-
'Don't you want to learn, and have to you knowledge cast?'

The girl spoke-
'If by tonight, these mangoes don't leave my cane,
Then, sure enough, I won't have my today's grain.
I cannot now worry for anything more,
Any other pain, any other wish, I cannot but ignore.'

To this were words-
'I came here to make these mangoes mine
But I would like to add another line-
For each mango, whatever you quote,
That you have, but a thousand times fold!'

On the girl's face appeared, that long due smile
This meant, closer to her dreams, she could move a mile.
An act such as this, so tender and sweet,
Instils hope, that spite and malice, we can defeat.

SOS Note #15

Written after reading an article about the same story during those testing quarantine times.

Poem 25
Visionary

The ones that make paths of light,
In dark or at times of fright
Surging solitary with all their might,
They make and hold the world upright
To them I wish to say-
'I owe you the dawn of the day.'

They, their spirit indomitable,
Leave their inspiring mark inimitable
Around the world and round the clock they work,
With their every word, they rouse a young Turk
To them I wish to say-
'I owe you the dawn of the day.'

If in thy heart, the lamp has been lit,
And there is born, that change making spirit
If you sow the seeds of joy,
In every girl, in every boy
To you I wish to say-
'I owe you the dawn of the day.'

Poem 26
Paradox

You feel the world is nothing else,
But a vapid mixture of aqua land
But in mind the meaning smells,
As a castle of golden sand
The world is a top of browns and blues,
Made of stones of turquoise hue!
A dance of shapes of different skews
The world is not a word to say,
But song of lives in different ways
Life is a wheel of ups and turns,
A journey of mysteries in sweet milk churned!
None has lastingly won or lost,
This, fate guarantees, at any cost.
The world is not a word to say,
But song of lives in different ways.

Poem 27
Cookie

I wasn't as charming
As I was, while walking out the oven
Just a couple pints of white,
Lying tasteless, indolent and away from the sun.
Once I came out, oh I didn't like it at all,
Those humans downed me in a sieve and shaped me to a ball!
I was bathed then, with oil and milk,
Perfumed with vanilla, and made as smooth as silk
There was company, I won't deny
Soda stuck by me and chocolate wasn't shy
Then there was pulling,
And I became few
Little sweet pieces, looking out for the next cue
Then came the worst, oh dear
We smouldered, while the earthlings made cheer
I didn't know chocolate was weak,
She melted, and hid through my creeks
After the ordeal, I came out,
I looked handsome, and smelled sweet no doubt!
Adored by the gleeful smiles around me,
And I am told, I make a great pair with tea.

SOS Note #16

Had to put down the recipe.

Poem 28
Perspective

Never something one knows,
Until at a crossroad, or a fix, else an uncertainty that grows
It is your weapon,
The strongest in your fate
Made with the metal of your beliefs and hate
Knowledge is its hilt, sentiments cleanse its blade new,
And hence discrete, in every one of you.
It can make you believe all's right,
Else coerce you to believe you are in dark's infinite night
Ergo be wary of how you make it grow
Let not your own weapon, end you at your low.

Poem 29
Counting The Infinite

Can you count infinite?
We all did, when young we were
Don't tell me you never tried,
To count the sparkles in the starry sky.
Deny not you never numbered
The slender strands that make your locks.
As you looked through the crystal clear creeks,
Tell me not you didn't tally those hued, swift fins.
But, an answer, we never found
We found something better-
Ourselves.
Infinite inspired to explore
Asked you never to keep your questions veiled;
When you gloat your triumphs,
It shows there is always more!
Thus our innocence matured in this endless quest,
A quest to know the form your soul is the best.

Poem 30
The Unbreathed Air

Some air has been in us, more often,
It's called home.
Teasing the same blue curtains and the same
warm kitchen;
Every second, runs through our blood, manifests
as comfort.
Often, or not, we breach this solace,
To the unfamiliar, unacquainted
Every hair, every cell of our skin sings,
invigorated;
It's novel, something they didn't have
The salt-laden air of the coast,
Wraps round like a fresh warm quilt
Crystalled invisible drops of water,
Hiding with the mountain winds fashion an
olfactory oblivion!
Unearthly sugared scents
Of the valley, from blooms known unknown
Makes you write poetry
Burning camphor and jasmine
From temples of yore,
Sink in your heart and the world you let go.

Poem 31
The Song Left Unsung

Pondering of your charm, from morn I sat
Rain, gale be it, you would come knew I.
As years passed without a look, neither a
rendezvous,
Drained not from my eyes, the hope of seeing
you.
Hours we used, still make my heart glad,
You coloured our eves, with your clever gaze
and long ballads!
Undone from the present, time strung these
pearls in the thread of past,
Minstrel of our melody, didn't apprise, that day
would be our last.
Nay, you shall come, though we may have
parted long,
And I shall wait for you to complete our
unfinished song.

Poem 32
Untold

I did not see you the first time you walked
through the door,
I did not feel you all the while you sat right
behind me.
Didn't see your love, even though your smile
said it all
I cannot fathom why you kept your heart untold.
Days passed and a year, we exchanged words
and maybe grew near.
You gave me your love, I took it, and in me,
your seed grew to a tree
I erred by raising that tree curtained from you
Else it would have been 'we' and not I and you.
A tree, so strong.... solitary....it has stood all
these years
Woe....why were we adept at shielding what was
pure and flaunted silence that was cold
And due to time's play.....it was my turn to be
untold.

Poem 33
Words From A Book Bought Again

I went to a home I never knew,
Sometimes sat still or with the wind I blew;
Curious hands ran through my fresh sheets,
And sometimes even fed coffee and sweet treats!
One day I left, I don't know why
To start a new life, I was told to try.
Having a new master was my yearly system,
As my pages browned, of the world, I gained
mysterious wisdom.
Now in your hands I rest, the same curious ones
For my stories, you can give a voice, or like the
rest, keep mum.

SOS Note #17

Felt the twenty or so books I hoarded from Blossoms (a bookstore I frequent) that day had thoughts.

Poem 34
Our Times

We knew our times
Dull people rest-
Foundations of wonder are swiftly passing
away;
Honest men are yet unsung,
A poem, not found, in my countrymen I seek.
Wit of centuries we adhere, unchanged
Difficulties, not enough to concern hardworking
souls
Eternal for years, all desires express themselves
The orator, in present, hears a beckoning,
With wonder, more he says-' God is in me'

SOS Note #18

A blackout poem.

Poem 35
An Unplanned Destination

A man once trod the soil, all ignorant and naïve
His path of life was unborn, a path he had to pave.
He had small eyes and small face,
And limbs that had not much pace.
But unfathomable power rested in him, unknown
The power to wonder was the divine gift that was sown.

He looked up to the sky and looked around,
He slowly began to break the chains of ignorance he was bound.
Thus man had lit the first lamp
And moved a mile on nature's endless ramp.

With the blazing torchlight clutched in his hand,
He walked on and on learning nature's laws
And realized he could reign supreme o'er the ones with claws.

He spearheaded his rise to power,

Forever resolving he would never cower.

And there was lit another lamp,
Another mile moved on nature's endless ramp.

As he triumphed through time,
He was draped in the silkened garbs of wisdom.
Making one and all grow, in his newly formed kingdom.
With his fellow's hearts and power on his shoulders borne,
The man moved from stone to throne.
Another lamp burst into man's will-fueled flames,
Nature bearing her creation's visionary aims.

He discovered what was undiscovered,
Piercing the skies, his knowledge powered.
He saw those that were unseen
He never returns being the prey or the animal he had been.
But, unknown to all, another seed had been sown,
Never to stop and say, I have completely grown.
Man surges, lighting his way through scorch and twilight,
His lit lamps slowly leading to the coveted infinite.

SOS Note #19

The product of another light-hearted poetry duel.

Poem 36
Define Devotion

It is not a lucid word to say
Because it does not mean you just pray
A submission that has you empowered,
As long as you have your trust and faith
unbowed
It’s pious, but quick to burn;
If you look to barter, or ask something in return
Both fragile and strongest at the same time,
It plays a mellifluous tune in your heart's chime.

Poem 37
Then One Day

There was a time, not long ago,
When our lives just waded to and fro
Not knowing dark, not knowing fear,
All were merry, without losing tears.

Then one day, 'it' came!
And once it did, nothing was ever the same.
In the beautiful streets where life and joy
bustled,

Not even did the leaves dare to rustle!

Everyone was a prisoner, their souls locked in melancholy's prison,
Punished for nothing, neither theft nor treason.
'It' was cruel, 'It' was vile,
'It' even masked little children's smiles.

All people prayed, with every new day they befriended,
That 'It' would go away, and their trials would be ended.

They knew the day was close, with all surety,
That-
There would be a 'Then one day', about which they would tell all posterity.

SOS Note #20

A COVID poem

Poem 38
Yearning

Burned,
Stronger than the fiercest fires
Making every vein tremble and shake,
Channelling every cell to believe,
In the dream, that
The magnificent mind chose to make.
It was a flame that never died
But I deny not that it waned
Bore down by aches, sometimes, or
Pained words of one’s dear and one's nemesis.
At times it took long, or fleeting in some,
For the blaze to morph,
Into the phoenix it was born to become

Poem 39
Cold As The Sun

The sun to me was so cold,
When the dark scared me, to the other side of
Earth, went he, to parole
As I stepped out to hike, he let the raindrops
have their say,
When I went out to read, he bore his heat into
my day!

The sun is so cold, made the shadows yield to
his temptation,
And in winters, he takes an erratic vacation!
Burns the strongest and in the sky sits high,
'The sun is cold' I shall still reply.

SOS Note #21

A poetry duel product. I must say this one was quite challenging given the intriguing topic.

Poem 40
About A Monsoon Walk

I walked solitary, down the lane,
Majestically adorned by the drops of rain,
As the petrichor whizzed past my nose,
Off my accord, I skipped and danced on my toes.
Rain, mystic rain, what still do you have in store?
I, at your every display, yearn to yell encore!

As wonder drops rested on my cheek,
My ears savoured the koel's delighted shriek,
Puddles and puddles, I saw, every inch of the ground,
In I jumped, splashing water everywhere around!
Rain! O joyous rain! What still do you have in store?
I at your every display, yearn to yell encore!

Through my blissful sojourn, to nature so close,
I forgot that when I started, was sad and morose.
Ecstatic at heart and oblivious to the world,
Into my niche of joy, sans worry, I curled.

Rain! Godly rain! What still do you have in store?
I at your every display, yearn to yell encore!

The sky changed, presenting her freshly found radiance,
She flipped her attire from monochrome to prismatic brilliance.
I was stunned, my eyes were shunned
With sombre eyes and amazed face,
To the sky, I gazed, gazed and gazed.

Poem 41

I'll Go To Another World

She sat there still, on marbled stone,
Honed by flair, the best that was known.
Though she could praise, this evident artistry,
'I'll go to another world,' said she

Donning raiment of linen, fine

Every pearl, round her neck, tussled to shine.
Though having that, what most did not,
'I'll go to another world' she'd retort

Although the trees, lured her with their green
pleasance,
And the jasmine cajoled, using their charming
redolence
Wind, the envoy of the sweetest fruits, couldn't
change,
'I'll go to another world'- her word arrange!

She placed her trust in the pages below,
To ferry her to a world, where she hoped to
grow.

With passion, deep, and unfaltering gaze,
She stepped into her world, with dreams to
chase.

SOS Note #22

Ekphrastic poetry on a painting by Charles Edward Perugini.

Poem 42
An Ode To The Eye

In the chasm of the passing day
They won't, a single event, let decay.
The umpteen elements they accrue;
Are the bricks of your dreams, and the aims you want to make true.
If to be curious, they are clayed,
You'll be shown what's real and what's feigned.
To empathy and affection, they answer with a smile

And order to be curtained at anything vile.
When there is surfeit of gaiety or overwhelm,
Emotions typhoon, and they step to the physical realm!
Sometimes, with their will, eyelids have them bedecked
When they thirst to reminisce, relish, relent and respect.

SOS Note #23

When you go to a party and see many pairs of beautifully decorated doors to the soul, you feel you must write about them.

Poem 43
Soliloquy On The Hilltop

I looked aloft and roared aloud,
My voice looking to reach the great Magellanic cloud;
'Why for a man, have you, just two eyes allowed?
I need more', to the numen I cowed.

What can I do, what can I say
Before me was nature's flamboyant ballet!
From the hilltop, my eyes Frisbee away,
As my nose savoured air's freshly made sorbet!

The waning sunlight brushed past my cheek,
The array of ranges stood, boasting of every peak.
The sky's pink, orange, blue and the warbler's delighted shriek,
Here and there a rustle of leaves, as the fawn took a peek.

From every other corner, the brook displayed her cheerful dance,
As she scattered pearls of water, flowing down the green expanse.

The clouds adorned the space as God's freelance,
The heavenly sight, induced in me a hypnotic trance!

I know not how much wonder, this world has in store,
Every soul in search of art, from the hill, shall yell encore!
Each second of this blissful sojourn, in my mind, will remain;
Oh! The hilltop, the enchanting hilltop, I wish I come again.

Poem 44
Reflection - It Is You

It's charming, if you want it to be
Or lifeless and dull, all is what you see.
Your hair can be a rhyme, smile, a part of
moon's glory
Else, it can be a tale without a story
Ripples can be the pristine music, stones the
coloured stage and you have the trees rustle to
clap on;
But some static souls state-' It's just a natural
phenomenon!'
This echo makes you think, tells not what's
untrue
It whispers you're great, but also teaches you-
That as you look the Earth, and look back at
time gone by,
If you learn from your stories, you shall soar to
the skies.

Poem 45
A Woman With A Pen And Paper

Undaunted, refused she, to use the world's
typical cage,
As she ran her inked wand o'er the plain lifeless
page
The metalled tip balleted to the serenade of her
mind,
Her bold and passionate heart, fueled that grand
design.
Unfazed, she voiced stories that were for years
untold,
And shed fresh light on tales that had grown old!
The world somehow looked different through
her kind eyes,
More care, love and less of despise
She, an enchantress, giving life to even rain and
stone,
Will live on, for as long as in the sky, stars are
shown.

Poem 46
An Ode To The Teacher

An year ago, I sat, my eyes drooping
With the textbook in my hand, formulae jumping and looping
As I wrote them down, cursing Newton under my breath;
I thought-
What more than problems can physics giveth?
But the wise said- 'A teacher is the one that makes you see'
Sure enough, that's exactly what happened to me!
And suddenly, something that was drab and morose;
Was adorned with laughter, becoming very close.
He wanted us to climb one step high,
So that when we faced the monstrous tests, we wouldn't sigh
When I didn't get a sum right or forgot a minus sign,

He would laugh it off and wouldn't whine.
We learnt to see physics in the mundane,
Like holding an umbrella, rowing a boat or in every drop of rain.
But all play and no work, not at all for him.
If you did, he would be really grim!
He kept saying physics is sight, might and light
And I couldn't stop but think he was right
As I flip back the pages and recall this wonderful sojourn,
Having a taste of what was in the knowledge urn.
He had once said- 'Find a reason to love and learn a subject'
I have found mine, have you yours yet?

SOS Note #24

Penned for my physics teacher.

Poem 47
Winged Wonders - Birds Of Ecstasy

I found a feather beneath a tree,
The lilac beauty was a sight to see,
Every bit was from Aphrodite's veil,
Abandoned and alone, it was lying in my swale.

My head tilted up and looked around,
Hoping that the winged wonder would be found,
And right up the red maple,
Was a blue bunting with beak sable.

Determined eyes and tiny feet,
The messenger of Zeus had come with his fleet,
The blues with the red was a treat to see,
To the soul it was like bread with tea!

Suddenly there was a burst of plutonium,
The next second was complete pandemonium!
The flock of bluebirds flew abreast,
In the dawn sky, it looked like Iris manifest.

I wonder who made these units of ecstasy,
Was it Athena or Hero's heavenly recipe

These beauties quench us of every dearth,
Birds truly bring joy to Earth.

Poem 48
Pizza's Journey

It all began,
In a little Italian hamlet,
Stemmed in the inventive baker's thoughtscape,
Who knew not the intensity, of what was to come.
Oh, it was divine!
The aroma whiffed past the cobbled streets,
Numbing the senses, of every maid and every child;
Sent them floating in culinary ecstasy!
Before you knew, the dough had risen,
In every oven, in every kitchen.
Dressed with cheese and sauces myriad,
This savoury stood the test of periods,
Every faction, in the world,
Designed and tailored it to their need,
Without this delight, is every celebration incomplete.
Deny not, this bread has won your palate,
But it all began, in a little Italian hamlet!

Poem 49
When You Get What You Want

When the course goes precisely as you thought,
Everything you had played out in your head
But even better
Sprinkling perfection in every detail you
couldn't imagine

When all the things you love come together
So beautifully, so easily
Leaving no room for complaints
Your soul bursts, your heart fills
Everywhere you see, each and every scene
Buys its way into your mind's coveted
everlasting memories

Its confounding
How a few moments of flawless occurring
Outweighs any memory the mind might have
accrued
Over months, or sometimes years.

It is enthralling to give up control
All your senses ensnared, numb
At the same time, your thoughts running wild
Revelling in the moment, yet foolishly-
Trying to create the future

After all, this came true
There appear to be no limits to what can, is
there?

SOS Note #25

Sometimes things go exactly as planned and no one is happier than you. I believe all those small moments of perfection must be cherished.

Poem 50
To Mom and Dad

I started writing a poem,
But then, I stopped and mused
Because longer than the longest tale it'll take,
For me to sing my heart for your sake
So perfect, so stunningly resilient
Your souls younger than mine,
But your minds with wisdom of ninety-nine.
You made me believe I could rule the world
And pushed me, when in my niche I was curled.
You bore my silly squabbles
And earnestly listened, when my thoughts I
babbled.
So little I have told till now,
Smaller than the preface of the book of your life
But of all the phrases I could choose
There is only one to use
And that is ' I love you'.

CPSIA information can be obtained
at www.ICGtesting.com
Printed in the USA
BVHW052244140723
667259BV00014B/802

9 789357 698382